EXPLORE THE WORLD

PHYSICAL SCIENCE

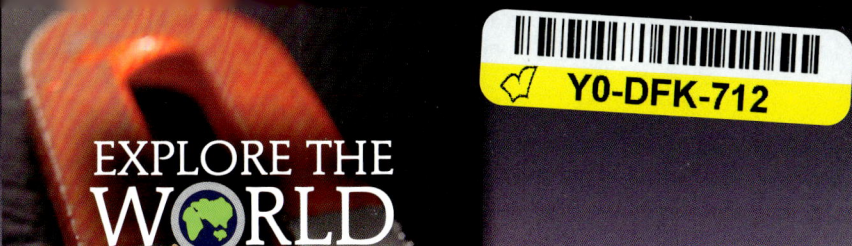

Life Is Electric

MICHÈLE DUFRESNE

TABLE OF CONTENTS

What Is Electricity?..2
How Does Electricity Move?.....................................8
How Does Electricity Get to Your Home?........10
What Are Fossil Fuels?...12
Renewable Energy..15
Glossary/Index...20

PIONEER VALLEY EDUCATIONAL PRESS, INC

WHAT IS ELECTRICITY?

Electricity is a huge part of everyday life. We use it to create light, heat our homes, and listen to music. We use electricity to cook and to keep food cold in the refrigerator. We use electricity to power phones, computers, and TVs.

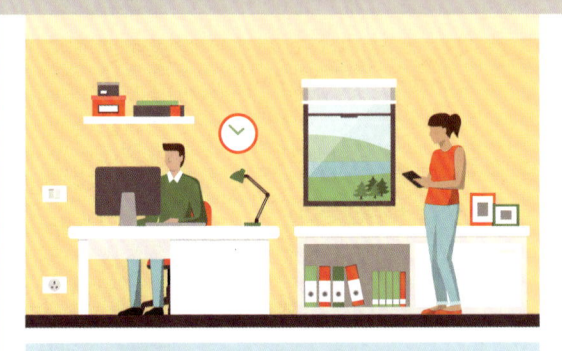

In 1752, **BENJAMIN FRANKLIN** did an experiment to prove that lightning is electric. The legend is that he flew a kite in a storm and waited for it to be struck by lightning.

Have you ever walked across a carpet and then touched a doorknob and felt a shock or tingling sensation? That is called static electricity.

If you rub a balloon on your head, the balloon will stick to your hair! Rubbing the balloon creates an electrical charge. The balloon gets a negative charge, and your hair gets a positive charge. They attract each other like the opposite ends of two magnets.

MORE TO EXPLORE

LIGHTNING is formed by the same static electricity that shows up in the balloon and hair experiment. Ice crystals and water droplets in clouds rub against each other and make static electricity. This energy is released as lightning.

5

Electricity is a force caused by small amounts of energy called electrical charges. These electrical charges exist in the **atoms** that make up everything around us. At the center of an atom is a particle called a **proton**. Protons have a positive charge. Other tiny particles called **electrons** circle around the edge of an atom. Electrons have a negative charge.

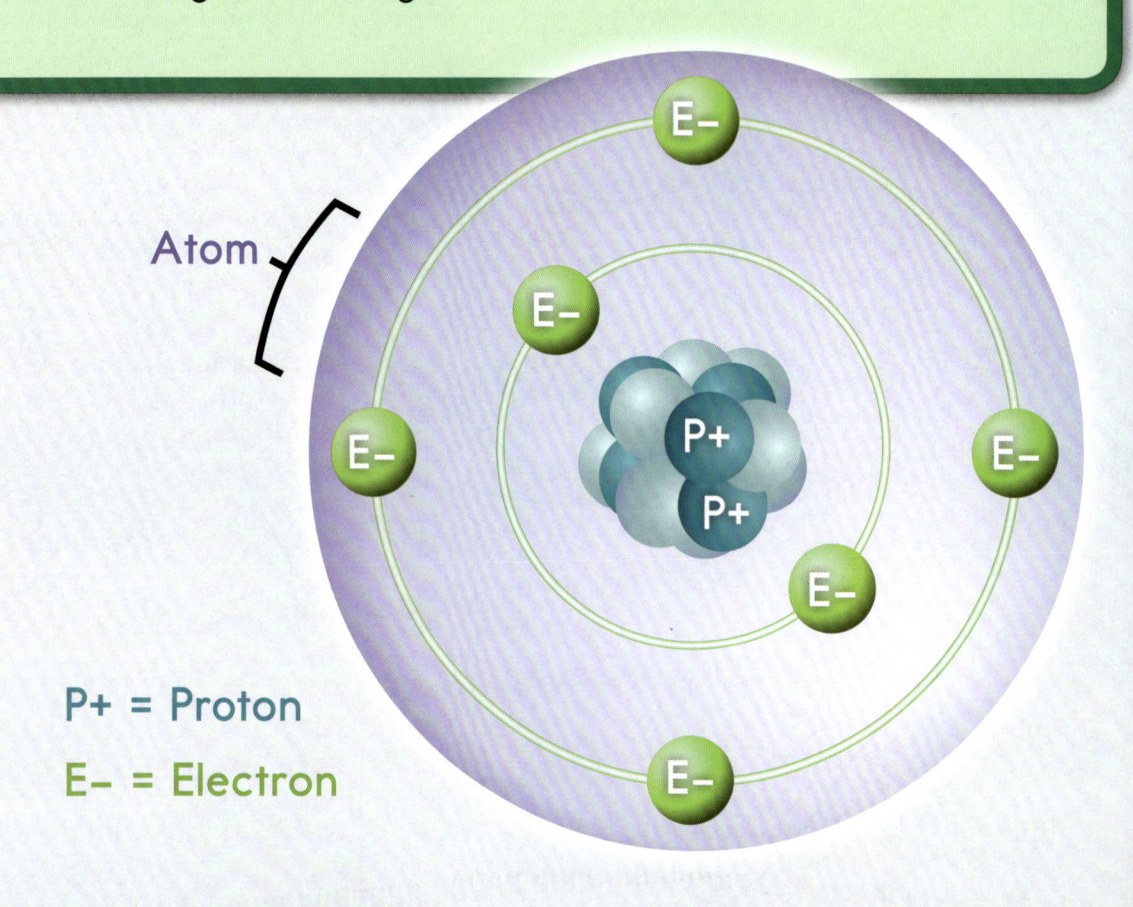

Atom

P+ = Proton
E− = Electron

6

Electrons and protons are attracted to each other. Some electrons stay close to the protons inside their own atom. Other electrons jump onto a different atom to get close to the protons of this new atom. This movement creates electrical charges.

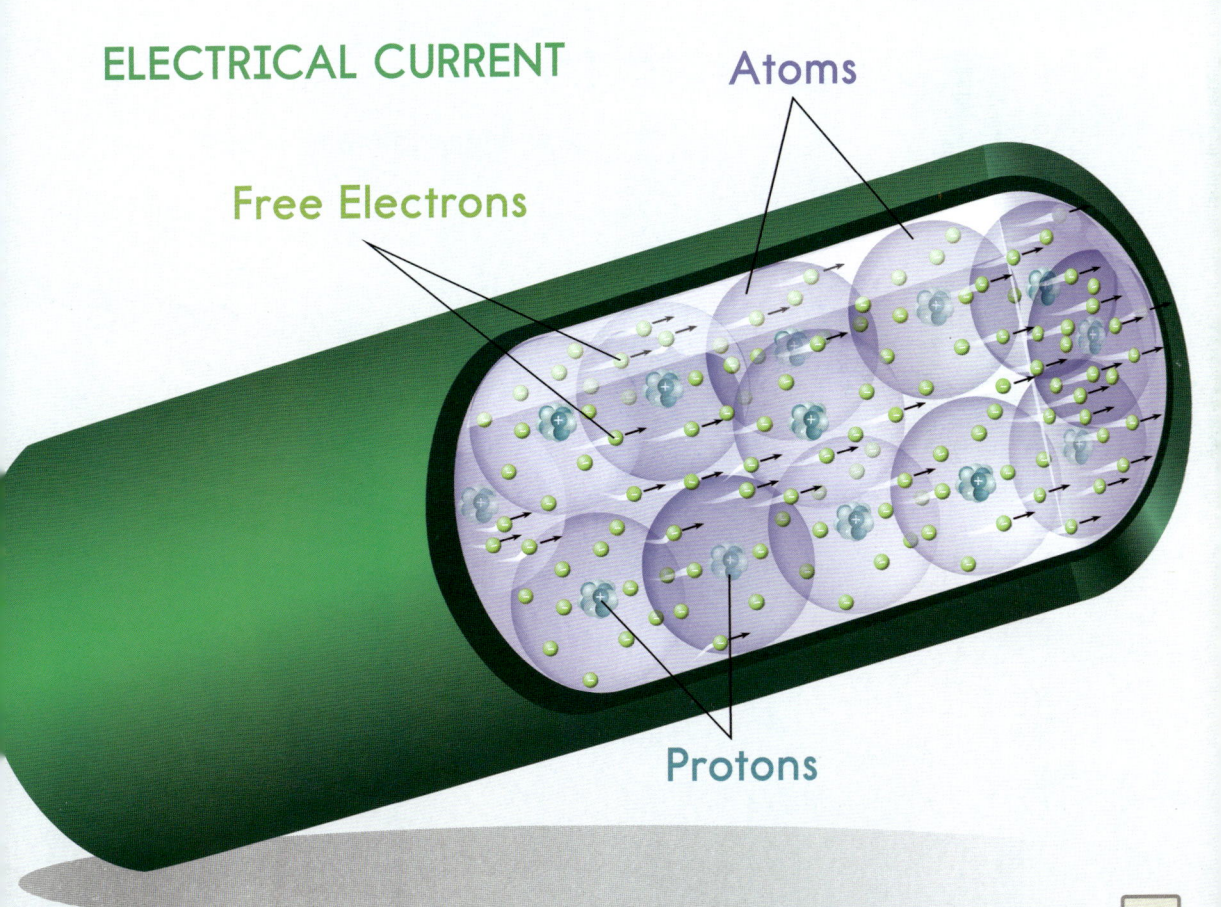

ELECTRICAL CURRENT

Atoms

Free Electrons

Protons

HOW DOES ELECTRICITY MOVE?

Electricity uses a simple loop to power things in your home. This loop is called a **circuit**. A wire carries electricity from a power source to the object being powered, and then brings the electricity back to the power source.

A switch turns the electricity on and off. The switch separates the wire when it is in an off position. When the switch is on, it pushes the two ends of the wire together.

When you plug a lamp into an electrical outlet and flip the switch on, an electric current runs through the outlet and up the cord. The electricity lights up the bulb in the lamp.

FLASHLIGHTS use a circuit too. They have metal wires that go from the batteries to the bulb and back to the battery, making a complete circuit.

MORE TO EXPLORE

9

HOW DOES ELECTRICITY GET TO YOUR HOME?

The electricity that we use in our homes usually comes from a power plant. Power plants are buildings that generate large amounts of electricity. Many power plants generate electricity by burning coal, oil, or natural gas. Electricity can also be made by **nuclear** power.

High-voltage lines allow electricity to travel long distances. The electricity is sent out from the power plants through thick metal wires to cities, towns, and homes.

11

WHAT ARE FOSSIL FUELS?

Coal, oil, and natural gas are called **fossil fuels**. We burn fossil fuels to make heat that creates electricity.

Fossil fuels come from dead plants and trees that lived millions of years ago. Back then, much of the earth was covered with swamps. As the trees and plants died, they sank to the bottom of the swamps and formed layers of a spongy material called peat. Over many hundreds of years, the peat was covered by sand, clay, and other minerals and formed a material called **sediment**.

Layers of rocks continued to form over the peat. As the layers grew heavier, the water was squeezed out of the peat. Once it dried out, the peat turned into coal, oil, and natural gas.

Using fossil fuels for electricity creates a lot of problems. One problem is that burning these fuels pollutes the air. Air pollution causes the earth to heat up, which affects our climate. This is called global warming. The overall warming of the earth could lead to rising sea levels, droughts, flooding, and more severe weather. Global warming is a challenge that we have only recently started to deal with.

Another problem with burning fossil fuels is that we could run out of them. Every year, we burn an incredible amount of fossil fuels. Not only do we use them to make electricity, but we also use them to run our cars and heat our homes. It takes millions of years to create fossil fuels, and we are running out of our supply very quickly.

There are **renewable** ways to generate electricity. These sources are constantly produced, so we will not run out of them as we use them. Renewable energy also produces a lot less air pollution than fossil fuels.

RENEWABLE ENERGY

We can generate electricity from the power of water, wind, and the sun. These are all renewable sources.

Using sunlight to power a building does not reduce the amount of sunlight in the world.

River water can rush through giant **turbines** that turn generators to make electricity.

The blowing wind can also turn the blades on turbines that create electricity.

Energy produced by the sun is called solar energy. Large panels called solar cells collect energy from the sun and turn it into electrical energy. There are many positive things about using solar energy. Solar energy does not create air pollution. You can easily put solar panels on the roofs of buildings to capture the sunlight.

SOLAR FARMS use thousands of solar panels to collect the sun's energy. The panels then turn this energy into electricity that can be sent out to cities and towns.

MORE TO EXPLORE

But there are some things about solar energy that make it less useful. The amount of sunlight that hits the earth's surface is not constant. It can vary depending on your location, the time of day, the season, and the weather.

Also, large amounts of space are needed to collect solar energy because the sun does not deliver very much energy to any place at one time.

Harnessing the wind is another way we can get renewable energy. Wind is probably the oldest source of power used by humans. Wind is clean, cheap, and renewable. We can draw energy from the wind by using large windmills with spinning blades. If we can capture enough energy from wind power, we can reduce our dependence on fossil fuels.

Not everything about wind power is positive. You need many windmills to generate a lot of electricity. These windmills take up a large amount of land. Noise from the windmills can disturb people living nearby. And when the wind is not blowing, the windmill blades do not generate any electricity.

MORE TO EXPLORE

Some people worry that windmills can kill wild birds. This was true of the early windmills but is no longer a problem. Today's **TURBINES SPIN AT LOWER SPEEDS** and cause very few bird deaths.

Many organizations around the US are switching to renewable sources of energy, including wind, water, solar, and more.

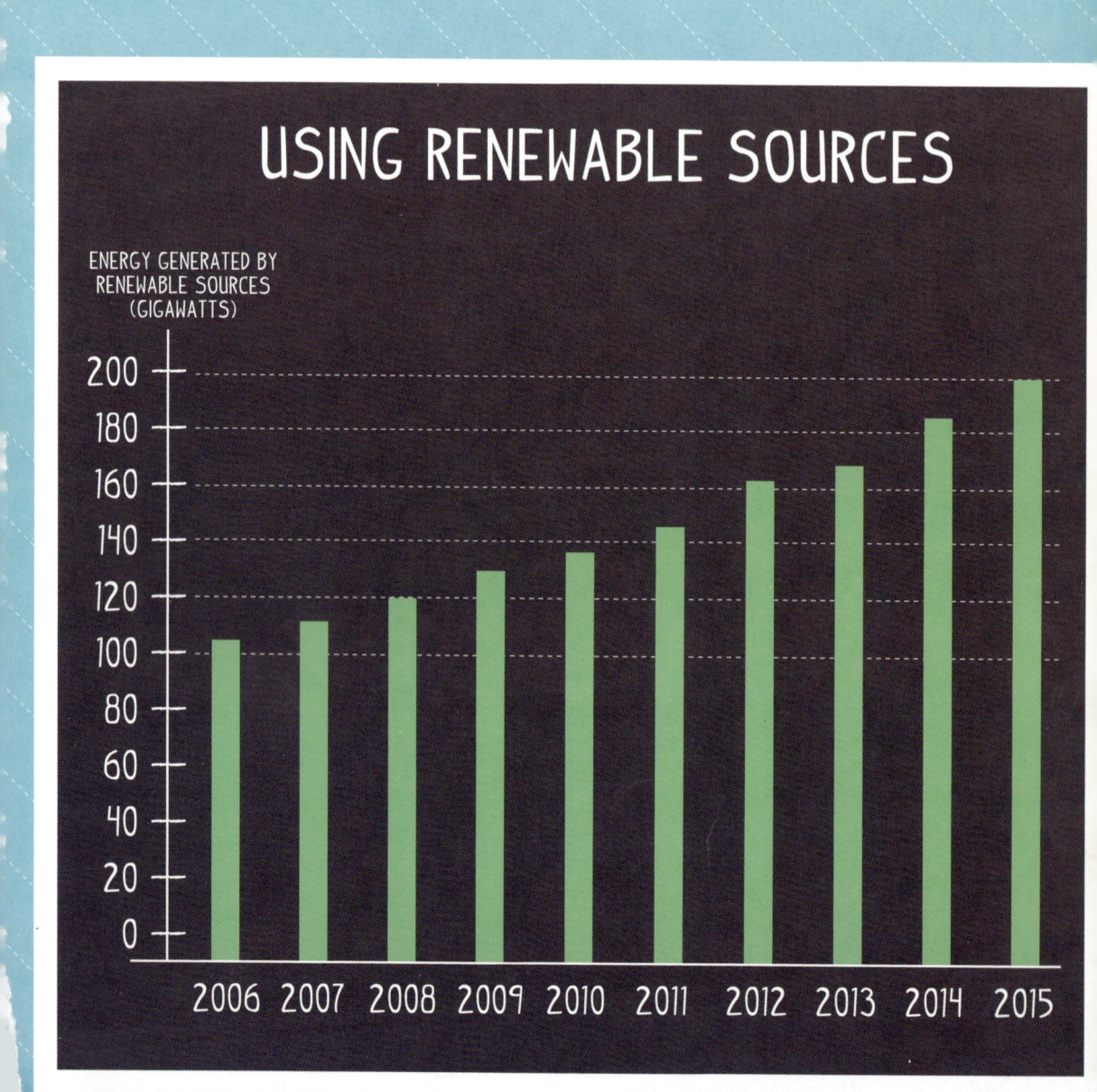

USING RENEWABLE SOURCES

ENERGY GENERATED BY RENEWABLE SOURCES (GIGAWATTS)

Year	Gigawatts
2006	105
2007	111
2008	120
2009	130
2010	136
2011	145
2012	161
2013	167
2014	184
2015	197

RENEWABLE ENERGY

WHERE OUR ENERGY COMES FROM

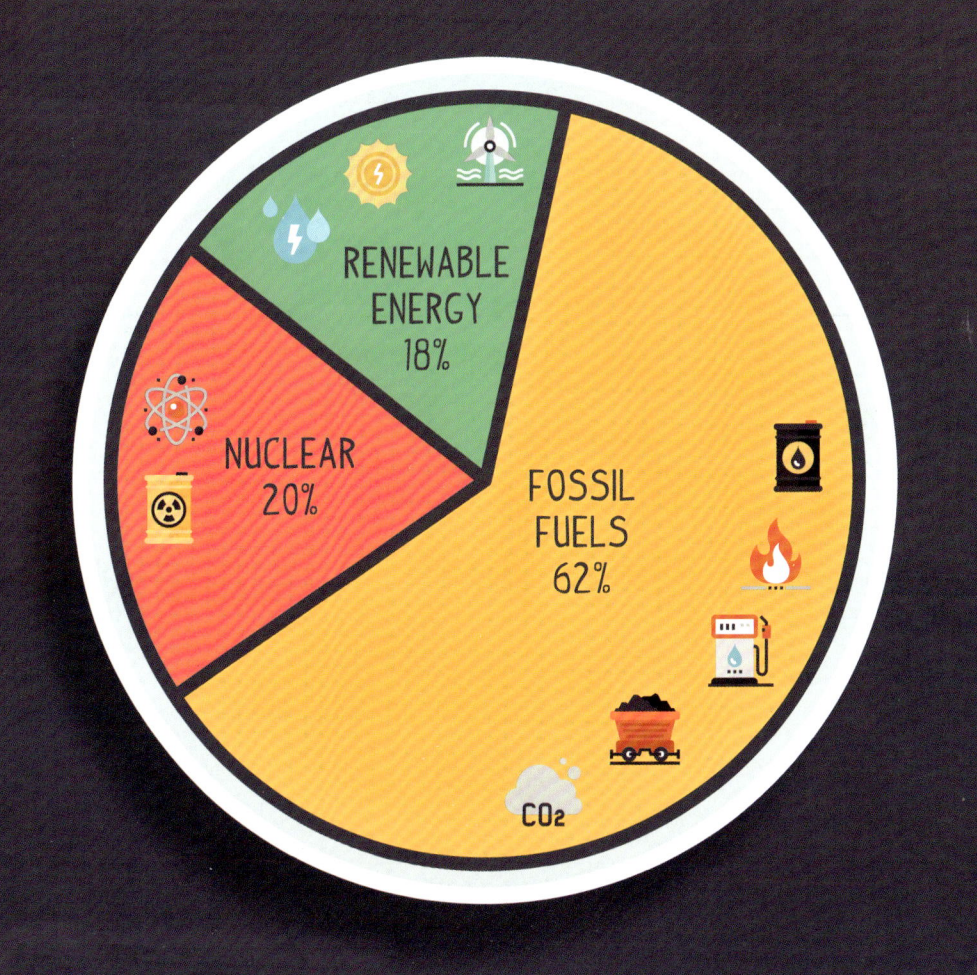

- RENEWABLE ENERGY 18%
- NUCLEAR 20%
- FOSSIL FUELS 62%

CO_2

GLOSSARY

atoms
the smallest particles that can exist by themselves

circuit
a closed path that electric currents travel through

electrons
particles outside the center of an atom that have a negative charge

fossil fuels
energy sources that are formed in the earth from plants and animals

high-voltage
having or using a very powerful flow of electricity

nuclear
reacting to an atom being split apart or joined together

proton
a particle in the center of an atom that has a positive electrical charge

renewable
restored or replaced by natural processes

sediment
something made from a material, such as stone or sand, that sinks down to the bottom of a liquid, is pressed together, and becomes hard

turbines
engines with blades that are spun by water, steam, or air

INDEX

atoms 6–7
batteries 9
Benjamin Franklin 3
blades 15, 18–19
circuit 8–9
climate 13
coal 10, 12–13
earth 12–13, 17
electrical charge 4, 6–7
electrical outlet 8
electricity 2, 4, 5, 6, 8, 10, 12–13, 14, 15, 16, 19
electrons 6–7
energy 5, 6, 14, 15–18
flashlights 9
fossil fuels 12–14, 18
global warming 13
heat 2, 12–14
high-voltage 10
lightning 3, 5
magnets 4
natural gas 10, 12–13
negative charge 4, 6
nuclear 10
oil 10, 12–13
particle 6
peat 12–13
pollution 13–14, 16
positive charge 4, 6
power plant 10
power source 8
proton 6–7
renewable 14–15, 18
sediment 12
solar cells 16
solar energy 16–17
solar farms 16
static electricity 4–5
sun 15–17
switch 8
turbines 15, 19
water 5, 13, 15
wind 15, 18–19
wire 8, 9, 10

20